HANDS · ON · SCIENCE

SPARKS TO POWER STATIONS

Kathryn Whyman

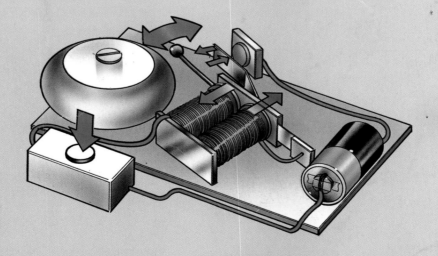

GLOUCESTER PRESS
New York · London · Toronto · Sydney

Contents

INTRODUCTION	4
SPARKS	6
ELECTRICITY FROM CHEMICALS	8
MAKING CIRCUITS	10
CONDUCTORS AND INSULATORS	12
RESISTING THE FLOW	14
HEAT AND LIGHT FROM ELECTRICITY	16
DIFFERENT TYPES OF CIRCUITS	18
ELECTROMAGNETS	20
ELECTROLYSIS	22
ELECTRIC MOTORS	24
POWER STATIONS	26
ELECTRICITY IN THE HOME	28
MORE ABOUT ELECTRICITY	30
GLOSSARY	31
INDEX	32

This book will tell you about electricity — from sparks to power stations.
Every page is set out as shown below with an introduction to science ideas, and "hands on" projects for you to do with simple equipment. There are also quizzes and there is a section about important discoveries at the back of the book.

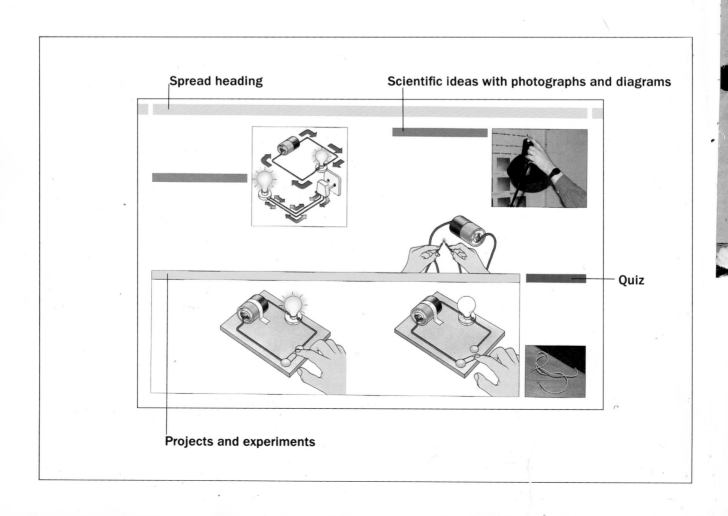

Spread heading

Scientific ideas with photographs and diagrams

Quiz

Projects and experiments

Introduction

Can you imagine life without electricity? What would life be like without television, lights, radios and record players? We take many of these things for granted yet many of the electrical appliances we use have only become widespread during the last 70 years. And in many parts of the world electricity from a power station is still not available. In these parts people still have to rely on fire for heat and light and animals for transport.

Electricity occurs naturally. For example, when lightning strikes there is a huge movement of electric charge. But electricity can also be generated. Large power stations across the country supply electricity to homes, schools and industries. These power stations generate enough electric current to light hundreds of millions of bulbs. You will find out more about what electricity is and what it does by doing the simple projects in this book.

Electric current travels along huge well-insulated wires

All things are made up of tiny particles. Some of these particles are electrically charged. This charge may be negative or positive. Electric current is a flow of negatively charged particles from one place to another. Sometimes you can see a flow of charge in the form of a spark. Lightning is a huge spark of electricity.

HOW DOES LIGHTNING STRIKE?

Lightning occurs when there is a gigantic flow of negative charge — or electricity. A flash of lightning is caused by huge amounts of electric charge leaping from one cloud to another. The diagram shows how the charge moves and produces sparks. Electric charge builds up inside a cloud when small drops of water and ice hit against each other. The bottom of the cloud becomes negatively charged compared with the ground below. This negative charge leaps from the cloud to the highest point on the ground, such as a tree. The huge flow of charge heats the air and produces the noise of thunder.

△ Lightning is extremely powerful. One flash can be seen from far away and can destroy trees, damage buildings and even kill people. The sound of thunder always follows the lightning flash.

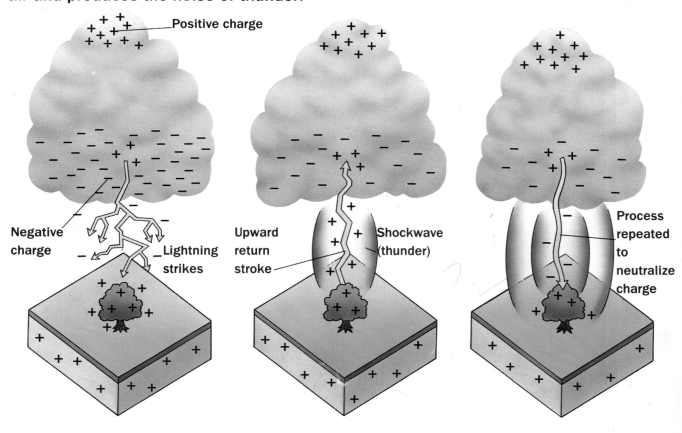

Positive charge

Negative charge

Lightning strikes

Upward return stroke

Shockwave (thunder)

Process repeated to neutralize charge

CHARGED CHIMNEYS

Industrial smokestacks often allow dirt and harmful chemicals into the atmosphere. This pollution can harm living things, including people, who need air to survive. Electric charges can be used to help cut down the amount of pollution which gets into the air. A layer of charged particles can be put on the inside of the smokestack. These charged particles pull particles of dirt (which are also charged) toward them and hold them inside. Like charges always repel each other — unlike charges attract each other.

LOOKING AT CHARGE

Electric charge which moves is called an electric current. But there can also be a build-up of charge which doesn't move and this is called static electricity. You can cause static electricity to build up by rubbing materials together. Charge a blown up balloon by rubbing it on your sweater. The charged balloon will pull certain things towards it. It can "bend" a thin stream of water.

△ The inside of this smokestack is charged to prevent too much dust and soot from getting into the air. If the smokestack is given a positive charge, then any dirt or soot with a negative charge will be attracted.

QUIZ

This boy is taking off his sweater. But why is his hair standing on end? And what are these sparks around his head? Try to explain what is happening. Does the same happen to you when you take off your sweater?

Balloon charged with static electricity can pick up small pieces of paper

Water "bends" towards charged balloon until it touches the balloon

Static electricity is not very useful for powering machines. Instead we use current electricity in homes and industries. An electric current is a *controlled* flow of electric charge. Batteries are convenient sources of current electricity that is produced from chemicals inside the battery.

HOW IT WORKS

A battery can be used to make an electric current when one is needed. Inside a battery there are two metal parts which are each covered by a special chemical. When the battery is connected to an appliance the chemicals inside the battery react with each other to produce charged particles. The negative charges collect at one end of the battery while the positive charges collect at the other. A stream of negative charge then flows round the appliance and back to the battery. As long as this current continues to flow, the appliance will work.

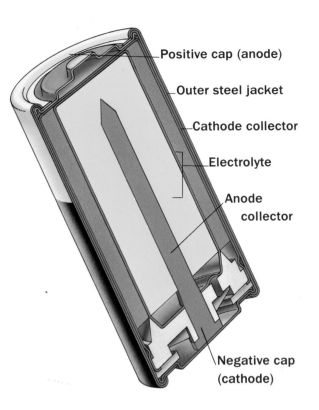

Positive cap (anode)

Outer steel jacket

Cathode collector

Electrolyte

Anode collector

Negative cap (cathode)

△ This is a simple battery negative charge flows from the positive end round the appliance, and back to the negative end.

USING BATTERIES

Flashlights, personal stereos and many other portable appliances need their own supply of current electricity. They get this supply from batteries. Batteries come in many different shapes and sizes depending on what they are needed for. Very small batteries are needed inside hearing aids and pocket calculators. Some batteries last for a long time before going "dead." The type of battery depends on the type of metals and chemicals inside it. The most common batteries use zinc and carbon but others use lithium, magnesium or lead. New types of battery are being developed.

▷ The photo shows some of the batteries now available. Batteries come in many different sizes — small enough to power a hearing aid, large enough to power a car.

RECHARGEABLE BATTERIES

When chemicals in a battery have been used up the battery is "dead" and no longer provides current electricity. Many batteries have to be thrown away at this stage. But others can be "recharged." This means that the chemical reaction which has taken place is reversed so the battery can be used again. Rechargeable batteries may last for a very long time and be recharged time and time again. Car batteries are rechargeable and it is possible to get small rechargeable flashlight batteries too. Some vehicles, such as wheelchairs, are completely powered by rechargeable batteries. Rechargeable batteries are less wasteful than others.

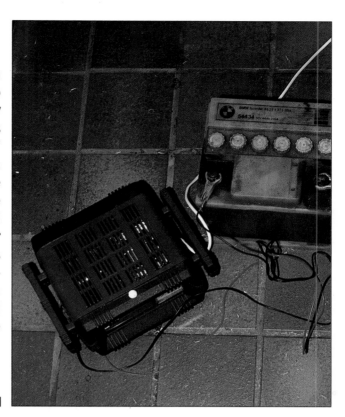

▷ Some car batteries are rechargeable. They can be plugged into the mains and recharged overnight.

MAKE SOME BATTERIES

Stick two pieces of metal that are different into a lemon. Make sure they do not touch each other. Connect a piece of wire to each piece of metal. Touch the wires onto your tongue (but not to each other). You will feel a tingle as a current is produced. Make a pile of copper and nickel coins. Arrange them alternately with pieces of blotting paper soaked in salt water between each one. Make sure the coins do not touch each other. Use your battery to light a flashlight bulb. You can attach the wires with tape.

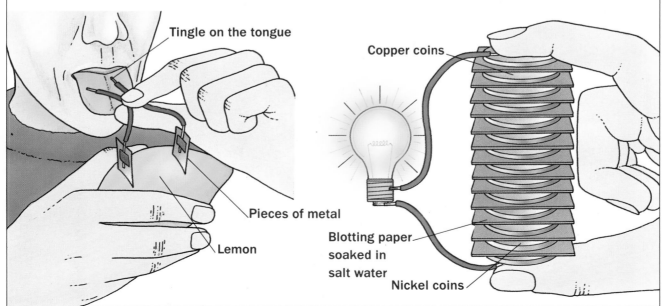

Tingle on the tongue

Pieces of metal

Lemon

Copper coins

Blotting paper soaked in salt water

Nickel coins

The path an electric current takes as it flows is called a "circuit." In a simple flashlight the circuit is made by the two wires, the battery and the bulb. Electric current flows from the battery to the bulb along one wire. As long as there are no breaks in the circuit, the current will flow and the bulb will stay lit.

TYPES OF CURRENT

The electric current that flows from a battery always travels in the same direction. This type of current is called direct current (DC). But most of the electricity you use comes from the supply lines from the power station. This current is constantly changing direction — backwards and forwards. It changes direction as often as 50-60 times per second. It is called alternating current (AC). AC is used for the mains supply because it can be transmitted more cheaply that DC. For most purposes AC is more efficient.

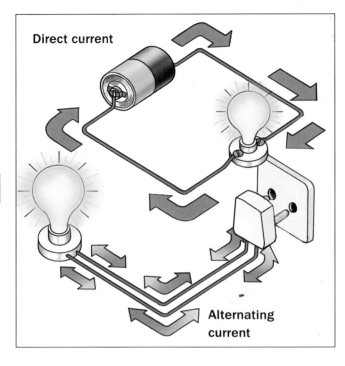

Direct current

Alternating current

△ The bulb in your flashlight is powered by direct current from a battery. But the lights in your home receive alternating current from the mains. You cannot tell by looking at a bulb if it is powered by AC or DC.

MAKING A CIRCUIT

The diagrams show you how to make your own simple circuit. You will need to use insulated wire which has had the plastic removed at each end — ask an adult to help you prepare the wire. The paper clip forms a switch. When the switch is "on" the bulb should light. If it does not light, check that there are no breaks in the circuit. To turn the bulb off, move the paper clip to the "off" position as shown in the diagram. Moving the paper clip breaks the circuit.

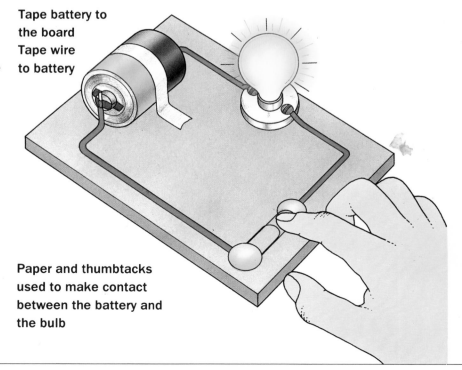

Tape battery to the board
Tape wire to battery

Paper and thumbtacks used to make contact between the battery and the bulb

SWITCHES

A switch is simply a way of breaking a circuit. All electric appliances are fitted with a switch so that they can be turned off when they are not in use. When a switch is turned "on" the circuit is complete and the current flows. But when a switch is put in the "off" position, a gap is made in the circuit. However the gap made by the switch needs to be quite large. The diagram below shows what can happen if the gap between two wires is too small — a spark of electricity may jump between them.

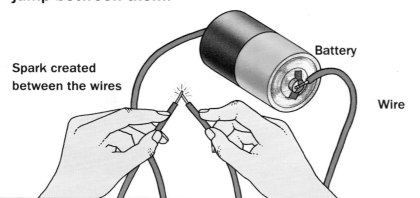

Spark created between the wires

Battery

Wire

△ Look around you and notice just how many things are operated by pressing a switch. In the "off" position a gap is made in the circuit. Electricity does not flow easily through the air in this gap, so the current stops. If the gap is very small, the electric current may jump between the two ends. This is what happens when there is a bad connection.

QUIZ

These trailing wires do not work properly. Why not? They are also dangerous. Can you suggest how they might give someone a shock or even start a fire? If you see a loose wire like this you should tell an adult so it can be fixed.

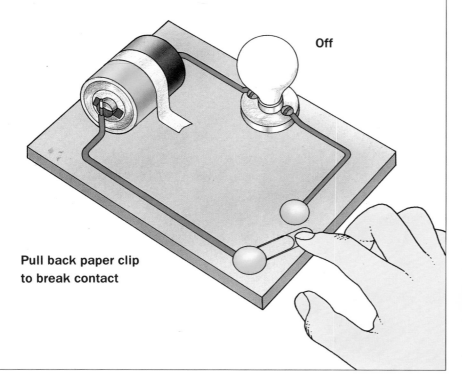

Off

Pull back paper clip to break contact

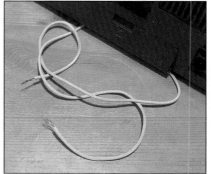

Electricity flows through some materials very easily. These materials are called conductors. Metals are good conductors of electricity. But electricity cannot flow through other substances, such as wood and plastic. These materials are insulators. Conductors and insulators are used for different purposes.

GOOD CONDUCTORS

All metals conduct electricity. The best metal conductor is silver which is used in circuits in computers. But silver is expensive. The best low cost metal conductor is copper. The power lines supply electricity along copper wires. Water is a weak conductor of electricity — but you should not touch electric appliances with wet hands or you may get a dangerous shock. The best conductors of all are known as "super conductors" and can conduct electricity at very low temperatures. These materials are only now being fully developed but may have a great effect on life in the future.

△ Cables are often covered with materials that do not carry an electric current easily.

▽ This tiny microchip circuit is made from aluminum which is a good conductor of electric current.

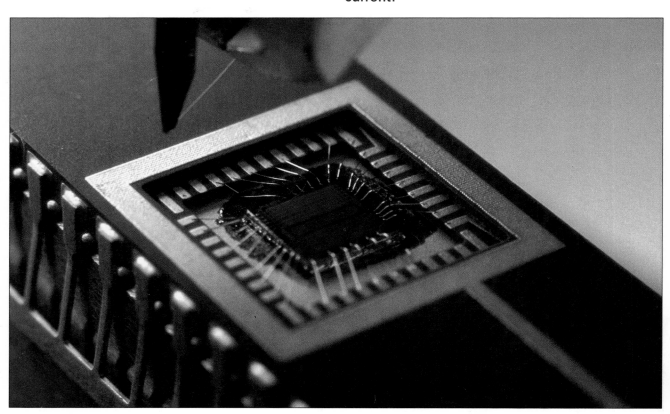

INSULATORS

Insulators are used to prevent electricity flowing where it is not wanted. You have seen how air acts as an insulator in a switch. The wires in household appliances are insulated from you and from each other by a plastic coating. Plugs and sockets are usually made of plastic or rubber so that you can touch them safely. Materials called ceramics also make good insulators. Ceramics are not flexible like plastic but can withstand very high temperatures. They are used in car engines and to coat electric oven rings so that you can cook without getting a shock through the saucepan if you should touch it.

△ Plastic is used to insulate wires as it is flexible and does not need to withstand high temperatures. Any break in the insulation could be dangerous and should be repaired.

EXPERIMENTS

Find out which materials are conductors and which are insulators by doing the experiment below. Check that the bulb lights when you touch the two ends of the wires together. Then fix them well apart on the plate. Use a variety of objects and materials to fill the gap between the wires. You can test wood and different types of metals by placing them in the circuit. Those which light the bulb are conductors. Those which do not are insulators. Try dipping the wires in water to see if water is a good conductor.

Ceramic plates

Bulb does not light up

Bowl of water

Bulb lights up

Other things to test

Copper is a good conductor — it hardly resists the flow of electricity through it at all. But thin copper wire allows less current through it than thick wire. And the longer the wire, the more it resists the flow of electricity. Coils of wire or other pieces of poor conductors can be put into circuits to reduce the current.

RESISTANCE

A thick wire can carry more electric current than a thin wire — rather like a wide road can carry more cars than a narrow one. So a thin wire in a circuit resists the current and reduces it. A long wire has a similar effect, reducing the current flowing through it. The diagram compares *resistance* in a circuit to a blockage in a bicycle pump. To get air through a blocked pump you have to pump harder. One way to keep a bulb shining brightly in a "blocked" circuit is to use an extra battery.

△ This shows some typical resistors used in circuits.

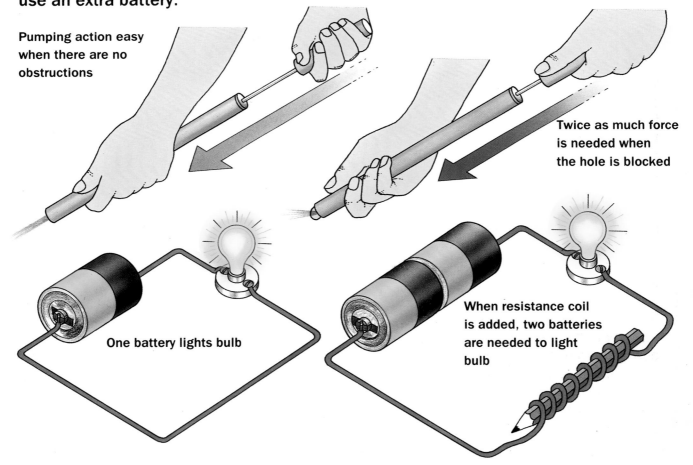

Pumping action easy when there are no obstructions

Twice as much force is needed when the hole is blocked

One battery lights bulb

When resistance coil is added, two batteries are needed to light bulb

USING RESISTANCE

Every time you turn up the volume on the television you alter the amount of current flowing in its circuit. The volume control is linked to a resistor made of a coil of wire. When the volume is turned up, less of this coil is included in the circuit so more current flows around it. The control for a toy car works in a similar way. When the lever is pushed in, less coil is included in the circuit, there is less resistance, and the car moves faster.

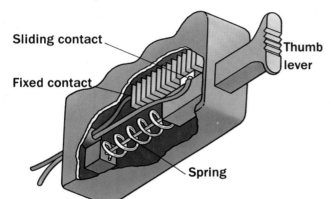

△ These children make their cars go faster or slower by changing the amount of current flowing through them.

MAKE A DIMMER SWITCH

You can make this dimmer switch. Use two batteries in your circuit and arrange them just as they are in the diagram — you may need to tape them together. Connect the wires as shown. As you move the free end of wire up and down the coil, you will find the bulb gets dimmer and brighter. When more of the coil is included in the circuit the resistance is greater, the current is reduced and the bulb glows less brightly. The amount of resistance depends on the size of the coiled wire.

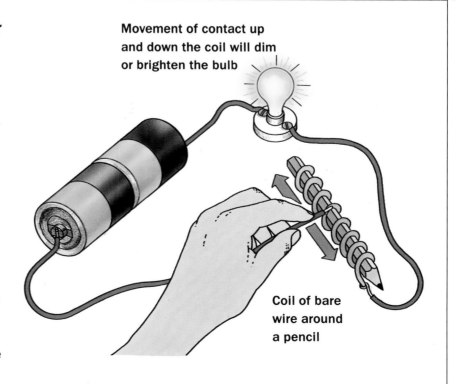

Movement of contact up and down the coil will dim or brighten the bulb

Coil of bare wire around a pencil

Heat and light can be produced by electricity. When an electric current flows through a coil of thin wire the wire gets hot and may also glow. Electric stoves, heaters and light bulbs all contain coils of different types of wire which give off heat and light as they resist the flow of the current.

INSIDE A WIRE

The diagram shows what happens when a current flows through a thin wire. A wire is made of billions of tiny particles called atoms. Atoms are made up of a nucleus that contains positively charged particles and electrons which each have a negative charge. When the electrons move in an ordered way, a current is produced. In a very thin wire the electrons bump into atoms more frequently than in a thicker wire. It is these collisions which produce heat when a current flows through a small space. Many electric heaters have a thin wire which glows when an electric current passes through it.

△ Inside this electric heater is a thin wire coiled tightly around an insulator. When the heater is switched on the wire gets red hot and the heat is blown into the room.

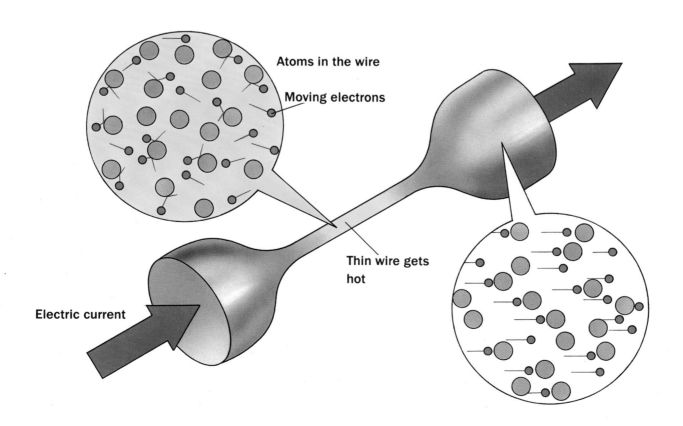

Atoms in the wire

Moving electrons

Thin wire gets hot

Electric current

LIGHTING UP

One of the most important uses of electricity is to provide artificial light. The simplest way to provide electric light is with a light bulb. When a light bulb is connected into a circuit it glows brightly. The part of the bulb which glows is called the filament. The filament is a coil of very thin wire made up of the metal tungsten. When electricity flows through the filament the wire gets very hot — as hot as 2,700°C. It glows white and gives out light. The filament is supported to prevent it falling inside the bulb. The hot filament would burn in air. So the bulb is filled with another gas such as argon. Some bulbs glow more brightly than others. The brightness of the bulb depends on the amount of current flowing through the filament. Light bulbs do not last forever — they are very fragile and easily broken.

NEON LIGHT

Not all electric lights use a filament. The neon light in the photograph is produced when an electric current is passed through a tube of the neon gas. The current provides energy as light. Different gases can be used to produce different colors of light. Neon makes red light, sodium makes yellow light and mercury makes blue light. Colored lights are not much use indoors. Fluorescent strip lights are used in offices to produce a whitish light. A fluorescent light works as an electric current is passed along the tube. This causes the atoms to move more quickly. As they stop moving, they give out white colored light.

△ Close-up of a light bulb filament. The coil glows when a current flows through it.

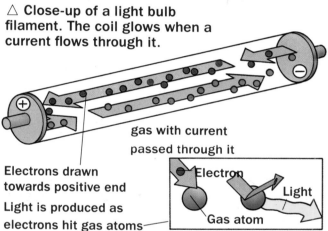

gas with current passed through it

Electrons drawn towards positive end

Light is produced as electrons hit gas atoms

Electron

Light

Gas atom

▷ Neon lights make very bright street signs and are a familiar sight in busy cities. Each color is achieved by using a different gas in the light.

A single battery may be used to power more than one bulb. The bulb may also be powered by more than one battery. When there are several parts to a circuit they may be arranged in different ways. The arrangement of bulbs and batteries in a circuit affects the brightness of the bulbs and the life of the batteries (how long they last.) There are two ways of arranging the parts — they may be in "series" or in "parallel." The choice of circuit depends on what it is used for.

SERIES AND PARALLEL

One simple way to arrange two bulbs in a circuit is in series. This means that the current flows first through one bulb and then through the next. When bulbs are connected in series the same current goes through each bulb. The more bulbs are connected into a series circuit the more dimly they glow. But if bulbs are connected in parallel they stay bright as you add more. If one bulb blows in a series circuit the whole circuit is broken so all the bulbs go out. But in a parallel circuit when one bulb blows the current can still flow through all the others which stay alight.

◁ Christmas tree lights are sometimes connected in series. This means that if any one of the bulbs blows the whole string goes out. It is better to have lights which are connected in parallel.

MAKE A TWO-WAY SWITCH

Two-way switches can be very useful. They allow you to turn the light on or off from two different places. You can see how they work by making this simple model. There is an alternative circuit included in the model so that you can turn the bulb on or off with either switch. The distance between the two switches would usually be much greater than in your model. Two-way switches are important for safety — they might be at the top and bottom staircase or at either end of a long corridor.

The diagrams show the two ways of arranging a circuit to light two bulbs. In the series circuit bulbs will be dimmer than in the parallel circuit. But the battery in the parallel circuit will run down more quickly because it supplys more current.

A bulb powered by two batteries connected in series will glow more brightly than a bulb powered by only one. Adding extra batteries in parallel will make the batteries last longer. You could set up these circuits yourself.

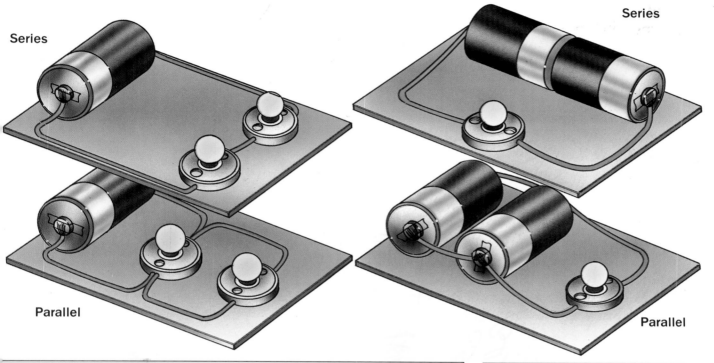

Series

Parallel

Series

Parallel

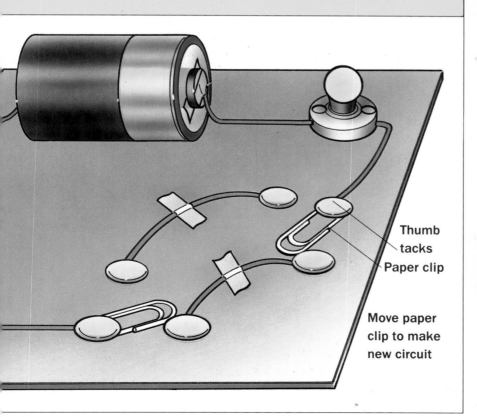

Thumb
tacks
Paper clip

Move paper
clip to make
new circuit

QUIZ

Suppose the lights on this tree are connected in series. What would happen to the lights if you removed one of the bulbs? Do you know why? Would the same thing happen if the lights were connected in parallel?

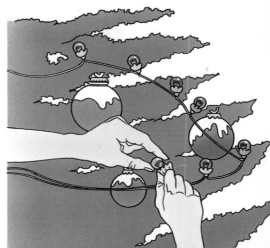

You can use electricity to make magnets. If you pass electricity through a wire that is wrapped around a core of iron, the iron becomes an "electromagnet." Like an ordinary magnet, an electromagnet pulls, or attracts, certain metals towards it. Electromagnets are used in many different circuits.

HOW THEY WORK

Magnets exert a special force. They pull objects made of certain metals towards them. An ordinary piece of iron can be made into a magnet by passing an electric current around it. This sort of magnet is called an electromagnet. An electromagnet is not a permanent magnet — when the current is switched off the iron core loses its magnetic properties. Huge electromagnets are used in scrapyards to lift and move metal objects. They are very powerful and can lift great weights. Much smaller electromagnets are used inside the circuits of appliances such as telephones, loudspeakers and electric bells.

△ Electromagnets have many uses. Because magnets attract certain metals, they can be used to separate scrap iron and steel.

MAKE AN ELECTROMAGNET

You can make your own electromagnet with some wire, a battery and an iron nail. Wind the wire round the nail, keeping the coils close together. The more coils you use the stronger the magnet will be. Join the wires to a simple circuit with a switch. When the switch is on your electromagnet will be able to pick up paper clips. When you turn it off the clips will fall off again and the nail will have lost all its magnetism.

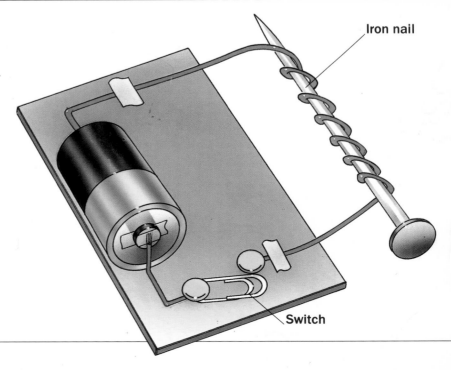

Iron nail

Switch

HOW A BELL WORKS

The diagram below shows the circuit inside an electric bell. When the bell is pressed the iron core becomes an electromagnet and pulls the iron hammer towards it, making it strike the bell. But when the circuit is broken, the iron core loses its magnetism and the hammer springs back. Once the hammer has returned the circuit is completed again and the process is repeated.

△ Press the bell and it will keep ringing. But once the circuit is broken the ringing will stop.

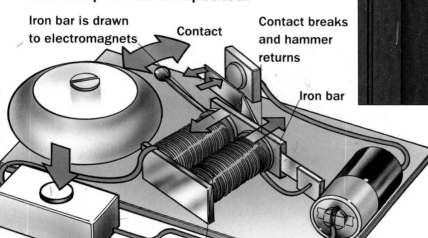

Iron bar is drawn to electromagnets

Contact

Contact breaks and hammer returns

Iron bar

Electromagnets

Battery

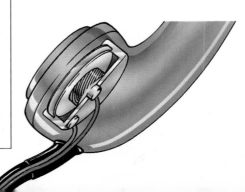

ON

OFF

QUIZ

Can you think of other appliances that use electromagnets to make a sound? The telephone uses an electromagnet to make a thin disc called a diaphragm vibrate.

In a battery chemicals react with each other to produce an electric current. But an electric current can also be used to cause chemical reactions. Electric currents can be used to split chemicals into the substances they are made of. This process is called "electrolysis." Electrolysis can be used to purify metals.

WHAT IS IT?

Electrolysis is a way of using electric currents to separate the chemical substances in a liquid. Some liquids are made up of positively charged particles and negatively charged ones. For example, when salt (sodium chloride) is dissolved in water it separates into positive sodium particles and negative chlorine ones. If a battery is connected to a cathode and an anode which are dipped into the liquid, the negative particles collect at the positive end (anode) of the battery while the positive ones collect at the negative end (cathode) of the battery.

EXTRACTING METALS

Aluminum is a very important metal that is used in cookware and electricity cables. But it is not found in its pure form. Instead it is found in a rock called bauxite which is a mixture of aluminum, oxygen and other materials. Electrolysis is used to get the pure metal. Molten alumina (aluminum and oxygen) is poured into a container. The oxygen particles are negatively charged and the aluminum ones carry a positive charge. When an electric current is passed through the liquid, the oxygen bubbles at the anode while the aluminum collects at the cathode where it can be removed.

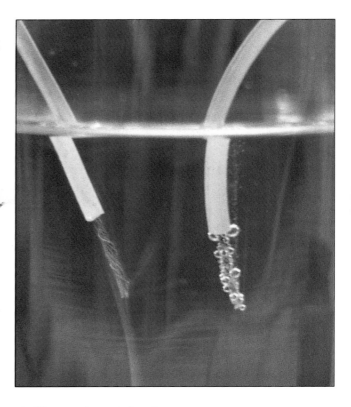

△ Charged particles in a liquid move when an electric current flows through it. The gas appears at the anode while the metal coats the cathode.

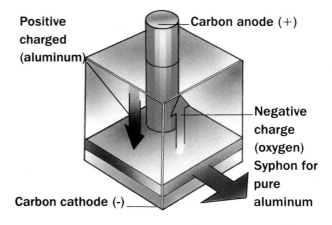

Positive charged (aluminum)

Carbon anode (+)

Negative charge (oxygen) Syphon for pure aluminum

Carbon cathode (-)

▷ Soft drink cans are often made from aluminum which has been obtained through electrolysis.

ELECTROPLATING

"Silver" jewelry or cutlery is not always solid silver it may be "silver plated." This is done by electrolysis. The diagram below shows how a piece of metal may be coated with a thin layer of another metal. It is attached to the negative terminal of an electricity supply and dipped into a liquid containing positive silver particles. When the current flows, the silver collects on the metal and coats it. This can be done with many metals. Iron nails are often coated with zinc to protect them from rusting.

△ Silver plating through electrolysis.

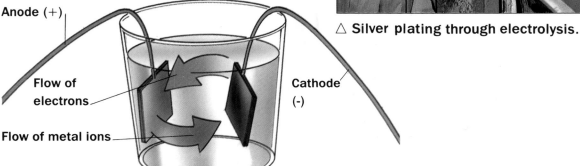

Anode (+)

Flow of electrons

Flow of metal ions

Cathode (-)

COPPER PLATING

You can copper plate an iron nail or disc. Attach a copper coin to the positive terminal of a battery. Connect a nail or iron disc to the negative terminal. Dip the coin and the disc into a beaker of copper sulphate solution. Positively charged particles of copper in the liquid will move towards the iron disc and coat it with a layer of pink copper. The bubbles around the coin are of oxygen gas.

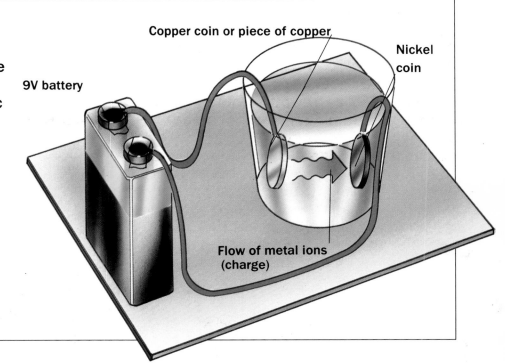

Copper coin or piece of copper

Nickel coin

9V battery

Flow of metal ions (charge)

The force exerted by a magnet can push or pull the charged particles making up an electric current to one side. When the current is flowing through a wire, the magnet makes the whole wire move. This idea is used in electric motors. An electric motor uses electricity and magnetism to produce movement.

HOW THEY WORK

The diagram shows how an electric motor works. In an electric motor there is an electric current in a coil of wire. A magnet is placed around the coil and this makes the coil move. In the drawing the battery is connected to a coil of wire which is in the shape of a square. The current flows up one side of the coil and pushes the other side up. This movement is repeated again and again so that the coil spins round and round between the magnets. Whatever is attached to the rotating coil – such as a food whisk – will turn with it.

△ When the motor is switched on, the coil spins round. This movement can be used to turn parts in a machine.

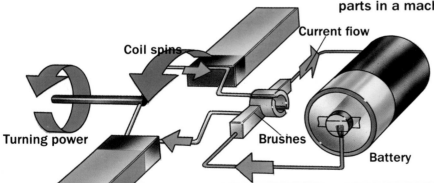

Coil spins   Current flow

Turning power   Brushes   Battery

▽ Many bicycles use a dynamo to power their lamps. As you peddle and turn the wheel, this movement is used to turn a magnet within a coil of wire to produce an electric current.

USING A DYNAMO

A dynamo is the opposite of an electric motor, almost like an electric motor in reverse. In a motor an electric current is used to produce a turning movement. In a dynamo, a turning movement is used to produce an electric current. So a dynamo generates electric current. A dynamo does this by turning a magnet within a coil of wire. Dynamos can be of many sizes depending on what they are to be used for.

MOTORS IN ACTION

The electric motor uses electricity to produce movement. There are many ways of using motors. In the home electric motors do all kinds of useful work: they churn water and clothes around in washing machines; and they turn the wheels in electric toy cars. Electric motors are also used outside the home: they can be found in underground trains, golf carts and escalators. You can probably think of many more examples. But all electric motors produce circular movement, ideal for turning wheels. Scientists are aiming to produce reliable electric cars to reduce pollution.

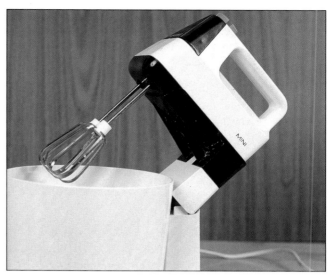

△ The moving parts in kitchen appliances are driven by electric motors.

EXPERIMENT TO SHOW AN ELECTRIC MOTOR IN ACTION

You can see the effect that a magnet has on an electric current by setting up this apparatus. You will need two small magnets, wire, tape, modelling clay a battery all connected together as shown in the diagram. When you turn the switch you should see the coil twitch — it is being pulled by the magnets.

The coil will not spin like a motor. This is because the current will keep flowing in the same direction rather than keep changing as it does in a motor.

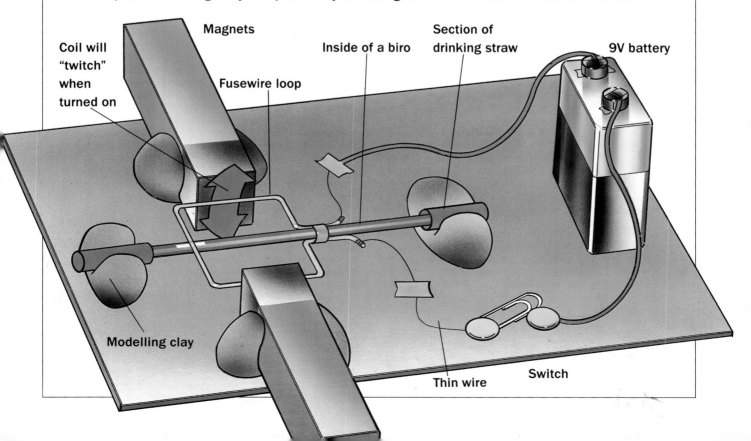

Coil will "twitch" when turned on

Magnets

Fusewire loop

Inside of a biro

Section of drinking straw

9V battery

Modelling clay

Thin wire

Switch

You have seen how an electric current can produce movement in an electric motor and how it is also possible to produce an electric current from movement. At a power station electricity is produced — or "generated" — by turning magnets at great speed inside coils of wire.

MAKING ELECTRICITY

The diagram below shows how the turning movement of a windmill can be converted into an electric current to light a bulb. The "generator" or dynamo is like a motor in reverse. As the windmill turns it makes a coil of wire rotate between two magnets. An electric current is generated which is being used to light a bulb. A dynamo like this can be used to power bicycle lights. In this case, the coil is rotated by the wheels as they turn. The electricity supplied to your home is generated in a power station in a similar way. However, in a power station it is the magnets which rotate inside a coil of wire. Moving the magnets in this way can generate huge amounts of current.

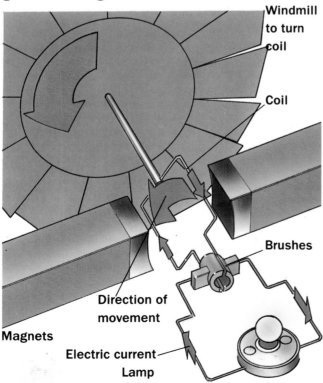

Windmill to turn coil

Coil

Brushes

Direction of movement

Magnets

Electric current

Lamp

POWER STATIONS

Power stations produce electricity on a large scale for homes and industries. Huge "turbines" turn magnets inside coils of wire to generate a current. A turbine is like a series of big wheels or fans. It may be spun around by steam or water. Steam to drive the turbine may be produced by using coal or oil to boil water. Or the energy may come from nuclear reactions. Once the electricity has been generated it must be carried across the country to where it is needed. These diagrams show how the turbine is designed to spin around.

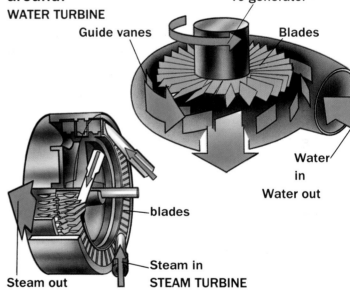

WATER TURBINE

To generator

Guide vanes

Blades

Water in

Water out

blades

Steam in

STEAM TURBINE

Steam out

▽ Energy from a dam of water or tidal barrier can be used to turn a turbine to generate electricity.

ELECTRICITY SUPPLY

Electric current is carried from power stations in thick cables. Some of these are buried beneath the ground and some are carried high above the ground with metal structures called pylons for support. A system of pylons and cables connects all the power stations in the country into one huge network called the grid. The diagram shows how electricity might reach your own town from the network. The electric power carried by these cables is very great. So, before the current can safely be used in your home, this power has to be reduced or "transformed" at a substation. The grid network allows power to be switched from one area to another as demand for it changes. If a power station fails, a local electric current from another power station is sent along the cables in the grid. This maintains the power supply in the area. In this way power cuts can often be avoided.

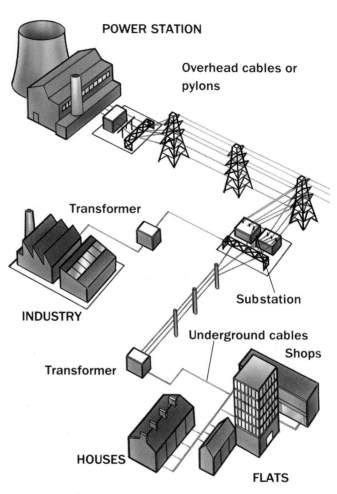

POWER STATION

Overhead cables or pylons

Transformer

Substation

INDUSTRY

Underground cables

Shops

Transformer

HOUSES

FLATS

PROJECT – MOTOR TO GENERATOR

Do this experiment to see for yourself how motors and generators are related. You will need to find two small electric motors from a toy car, for example. Connect one motor to a battery – it should turn. Switch the first motor off while you join it to a second motor. This should be connected to a bulb. When you turn the switch on, the first motor will make the second motor act like a dynamo. The current generated by the dynamo lights the bulb.

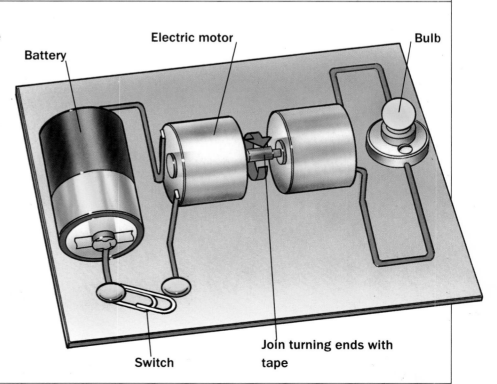

Battery

Electric motor

Bulb

Switch

Join turning ends with tape

You use electricity in the home for many purposes — to power lights, televisions, stoves, videos and much more. Electricity is supplied to two kinds of circuits in the home — the lighting circuit and the sockets. Electrical appliances are connected to the power supply by putting a plug into a socket.

APPLIANCES

An appliance is a machine that you use to do some sort of work for you. You probably use many electrical appliances in your home. Appliances may use electric power to produce light or heat; to drive a motor or to produce sound. Different appliances use different amounts of current. Those producing heat, such as a stove, use much more than those producing light or sound, like the television. Each appliance has a circuit that can be connected into the power supply.

△ Life without electricity would be very different. All of the appliances in the photograph need a supply of electricity to power them.

HOUSE WIRING

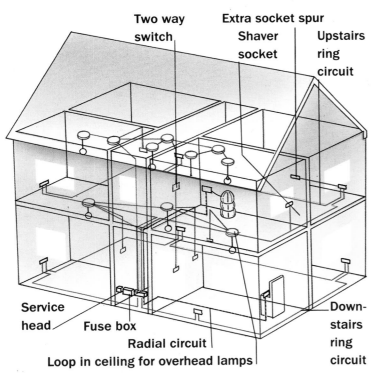

Two way switch

Extra socket spur

Shaver socket

Upstairs ring circuit

Service head

Fuse box

Radial circuit

Loop in ceiling for overhead lamps

Downstairs ring circuit

The diagram shows how electrical wiring is usually arranged in a house. Electricity enters the house through a wire, flows through the fuse box and separates into two types of circuits. One type of circuit powers the main lights. Other circuits supply electricity to the sockets. This runs around the house, usually between the walls or under the floorboards. At a number of places in each room the circuit opens into a socket. Appliances can be connected to the circuit at these sockets. The current flows into the appliance through one wire and then back to the "neutral" wire. The amount of electric current which enters a house is measured by a meter. This is a small motor connected to a counting device. A dial on the meter shows how much electric current has been used. In many countries, it is cheaper to use electricity during the night when there is less demand for power.

PLUGS AND FUSES

A plug carries wires leading from an appliance and connects them to the wires in the main circuit. Inside a plug there is a live wire (coated in black insulation) and a neutral one (which is white). The live wire carries the current to the appliance. The current returns to the power supply through the neutral wire. In some countries plugs also have a ground wire. The ground wire does not usually carry a current — it is there as a safety device. If there is a fault in the appliance and it becomes "live," or is connected to the power supply, the ground wire provides a route for the current to flow safely to the ground.

Most circuits carry a fuse or a circuit breaker. A fuse is a thin piece of wire included in the circuit. If too much currrent flows round the circuit the fuse melts and breaks the circuit before damage is done. A circuit breaker works in a similar manner, but no metal melts and the breaker can be reset after the problem has been corrected. The diagram shows how a fuse completes a circuit and how a blown fuse breaks it.

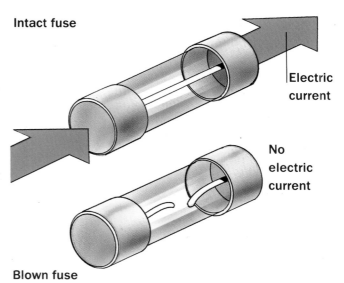

Intact fuse

Electric current

No electric current

Blown fuse

Machine has a ground wire for safety

QUIZ

Electricity is a very versatile source of power: it can cause light, movement and sound and it can be used to make things hot or cold. Look at the different appliances drawn opposite. They are all everyday items and they use electric current to produce different effects. Can you say what they are? Can you think of other machines that use electric motors to produce circular motion? How many different ways is electricity used in a washing machine?

The Greeks knew about static electricity — pieces of amber could pick up small scraps of straw. There have been many very important discoveries and inventions concerned with current electricity. On this page you can see some of the major ones — from simple batteries to complex telephone systems.

Volta presenting his battery to Napoleon

Volta and the battery

Count Alessandra Volta (1745-1827) was an Italian scientist. His most important discovery was in 1800 when he found that chemicals could be used to produce an electric current. He made the first simple battery by placing two discs, one of silver and one of zinc, into a solution of acid. When he linked the discs together with wire he found that electricity flowed through the wire. By using a pile of silver and zinc discs he invented the battery known as the "Voltaic pile".

André-Marie Ampère

Franklin and Ampère

Benjamin Franklin (1706-1790) was the American scientist who showed that lightning is a discharge of electricity. He tied the end of a kite string to a piece of metal on the ground and allowed the kite to fly during a storm. Lightning struck the kite and moved down the string to Earth.

André-Marie Ampère (1755-1836) was a French scientist. He was the first person to understand the importance of the link between electricity and magnetism.

Benjamin Franklin

The telephone

Alexander Graham Bell (1847-1922) invented the telephone in 1876. So did Elisha Gray but Bell beat him to the patent office! This telephone contained the first microphone which was based on an electromagnet. Since Bell's early design, telephones have become one of the most important methods of communication.

Alexander Graham Bell

Anode
This is the place at which negatively charged particles collect during electrolysis.

Atom
Every substance is made up of particles called atoms. An atom consists of a central nucleus surrounded by negatively charged particles called electrons.

Cathode
This is the place at which positively charged the process of particles collect during electrolysis.

Charge
Many of the particles of an atom carry electric charge. Inside the nucleus, protons carry a postive charge and the electrons carry negative charge. Positive and negative charges attract each other, but like charges, such as two electrons, repel.

Circuit
A complete path around which an electric current can flow.

Electric current
A flow of negative charge (electrons) round a circuit.

Grid
The national system which connects electricity generators, such as power stations, and users of electricity, such as homes, by cables.

Microchip
A tiny slice of silicon which has a circuit etched onto it. Microchips are used in calculators and many other electric appliances.

Static electricity
When certain materials are rubbed together, electrons move from one material to the other. One material becomes positively charged while the other gains a negative charge. The build-up of negative charge on this material does not flow anywhere so it is called static electricity. However, if the build up of electrons is great enough they may leap across to the positively charged material as a spark.

Substation
Electricity leaves the power station in a form which is too powerful for you to use. It is powerful enough to power hundreds of millions of electric fires. Before it reaches your home it may pass through a number of substations where the power is adjusted.

Superconductor
A superconductor is a material which does not resist the flow of electric current at all. So far the only superconductors which have been discovered only lose all their resistance at very low temperatures.

Terminal
The part of a battery to which wires can be joined. A battery has two terminals — one positive and one negative.

A
alternating current 10
aluminum 12, 22
ampere 30
Ampere, Andre-Marie 30
anode 22, 31
argon 17
atoms 16, 31

B
battery 8-9, 14, 15, 18,
    19, 20, 22, 27, 30
bell 20, 21
Bell, Alexander Graham
    30

C
carbon 8, 16
cathode 22, 31
charge 6-7, 8, 31
chlorine 22
circuits 10-1, 14, 15,
    18-9, 20, 21, 28, 31
coil 14, 15, 16, 17, 20,
    24, 26
conductors 12-3, 14
copper 12, 14, 23

D
direct current 10
dynamo 24, 26, 27

E
earth wire 29
electric current 7, 8, 9,
    10, 15, 16, 18, 19, 22,
    24, 26, 27, 30, 31
electrolysis 22-3
electromagnets 20-1, 30
electrons 16

electroplating 23

F
filament 17, 29
Franklin, Benjamin 30
fuses 28, 29

G
generators 27
Gray, Elisha 30
grid 27, 31

H
heat 16-7, 28

I
insulators 12-3
iron 20, 21, 23

L
lead 8
light 16-7, 28
lightning 6, 30
lithium 8
live wire 29

M
magnesium 8
magnets 20, 21, 24, 26,
    30
mains 10, 28, 29
microchip 12, 31
microphone 30
motor 24-5, 26, 27, 28

N
negative charge 6, 8, 16,
    22
neutral wire 29

O
oxygen 22

P
parallel 18, 19
positive charge 6, 8, 16,
    22
power stations 10, 12
    26-7

R
resistors 14-5
ring circuit 28

S
series 18, 19
silver 12, 23, 30
sodium chloride 22
static electricity 7, 8, 30,
substation 27, 31
superconductor 12, 31
switch 11, 19, 20, 24,
    25, 27

T
telephone 20, 21, 30
television 15, 28
terminal 31
tungsten 17
turbine 26

V
Volta, Alessandra 30

W
windmill 26
wiring 28-9

Z
zinc 8, 23, 30

Photographic credits:
Cover and page 20: Science Photo Library; pages 5, 6, 7, 12 both, 18 and 25: Zefa; pages 8 and 22B: Picturepoint; pages 9, 11 both, 14, 16, 22T and 28 Vanessa Bailey; pages 13 and 24T: Paul Brierley; pages 15, 21, 23 and 24B: Chapel Studios; page 17 both: Spectrum; page 30 all: Popperfoto.